Costumes Theda wore in *A Fool There Was* (1915), including a fringed shawl that exists today in a private collection.

Afternoon gown, fur and hat from *The Blue Flame* (1920).

The suit, cape and hat Theda wore to the Chicago premier of *Cleopatra*.

Low waist tea gown and robe from *When a Woman Sins* (1918).

Costume worn in *Salome* (1918), made by George Hopkins.

Princess gown from *Camille* (1917), possibly designed by Paquin.

Drop waist street dress worn in *The Eternal Sappho* (1916).

Costume by George Hopkins (Neje) for *Madame du Barry* (1917). The original dress survives.

Do not cut spaces between arms and dress.